Luminous Dream

by

Wally Swist

A Finalist for the 2010 FutureCycle Poetry Book Prize

FutureCycle Press
futurecycle.org

Published by FutureCycle Press
Cave Spring, Georgia, U.S.A.

ISBN: 978-0-9828612-1-9

"What a gorgeous book this is! Wally Swist writes of passionate love with a quiet grace that stirred this reader's heart. Each individual poem moved me deeply; as a whole, *Luminous Dream* simply knocked me out. Shades of Pablo Neruda, Mary Oliver, and Gary Snyder abound, yet the poet's voice is uniquely his own. This is a book I will return to again and again with deep pleasure."

— Lesléa Newman,
author of *Nobody's Mother* and *Still Life with Buddy*,
Poet Laureate, Northampton, MA 2008-2010

"These poems are a beautifully perceptive reading of both the natural world and ourselves as its necessary testament and witness. If 'seeing is believing,' then Wally Swist can make believers of us all."

— Robert Creeley

"Wally Swist's poems are full of clean perceptions and clear, proportionate feeling. They are easy to read in the sense that they are continually rewarding. They have a fine balance, doing justice to the natural, the human, and the divine, and treating none of these as refuge from another. As a grateful reader, I applaud him."

— Richard Wilbur

Dedication

In finishing these poems — as finished as
any poems will ever be — they are no longer
mine, and so I dedicate this book to every
reader of these poems. The poems are yours,
written upon the same premise and in a similar
spirit as their original source of literary
inspiration, a book I came upon in my youth
and still cherish, *Veinte poemas de amor y una
cancion de desesperada* by Pablo Neruda.

Contents

Active Grace

We speak of the challenge of being able to articulate bliss.
She brings about rapture in me whenever we are together.

It is my experience that it is not just energy,
that it is not pedestrian, that it perpetuates itself between us.

I find this consistent and beyond any expectations.
We both seek *Atman* and *Brahman* in ourselves, although

I find sustenance, without dogma, a touchstone within her.
Something as rhapsodic as this can be heard

in the music of Brahms's *Variations on a Theme by Haydn.*
In the rigors of something that beautiful resounding

across the keyboards of two pianos on the CD player,
I go back to it, then not getting enough, go back again.

Aftermath

We talk cautiously of differences: how the fragrance of roses
opens in the heat of the afternoon, how honey locust blossoms

are most fragrant in evening coolness, how the shape
of the beech leaf opposes the chestnut, the first saw-toothed,

the latter elliptical, notched, the tips tapered.
We remark how ferns have uncurled their green fists into
    fronds.

We walk back into the meadow, find patches of strawberries
we pluck by the handful. You dispose one after another

into my mouth. The tart sweetness sears my tongue.
Beneath the bluest possible sky, the whole field burns with
    blossoms.

All the Green Lights Going Home

Back on my feet again and summer already.
The third floor apartment sweaty and hot,

but there's money finally coming
to pay the rent, stock groceries

on the pantry shelves: I found work.
Back on my feet again, driving through

a city summer night; headlights slice
the air, stringing a breeze like paper dolls

through rolled-down windows.
Back on my feet again. Her head cradles

snugly on my shoulder, rocking against
potholes and bumps. Fingers rain dance

over her ankles to the radio's pop,
and I make all the green lights going home.

Alone

The sky, when she laughs, unties necklaces
of pearls. Tomorrow, we will wake up

with each other. We will be
more alone than anyone else in the world.

And She Falls into My Arms Again

He calls.
He calls in the morning.
He calls in the middle of the afternoon.
At night he calls.

I know the position he's in.
I've been there once or twice myself.
You call your lover.
You call your lover on the phone.

You write her letters that go unanswered,
Bang on her door at midnight.
When she finally hangs up,
I always have to ask: *Who was it?*

It was him.
What did he want?
Oh, you know.
And she falls into my arms again.

Anima and Animus

When you ask me to tell you that you will never have
anyone else, repeatedly telling me to say it again

and again, I look at you and see you are wearing
my face, and you look at me and see I am wearing yours.

Anniversary

Walking together on our anniversary in this garden
dedicated to Buddha, the well chiseled into rock

is filled with rainwater, sky, azalea blossoms.
We recollect most of what happened that first night:

what we said, what we did, how the rippled current
of the river flowed past the budding maple

branch dragging in the water. When we return
to the gazebo, the wood looks weathered. It is

smaller than we recall; the bench on one side broken
on the floor. We spread out our bread and cheese.

When we eat, every moment matters. Hours later,
when I blow out the candle, the smell of melted wax.

The Anointing

I think of the lacy trickle
of the falls, as I anoint you

with kisses, climbing down
sweet ledges of your body

from your lips to your breasts,
then, going beyond

to the mossy pool below,
my tongue duplicating

the rhythm dimpled by
the sprinkling of summer rain.

The Ascent

Ascending the trail, the heat
haze shimmers from ledge to pool

and from pool to ledge of the stream,
my forehead beaded with sweat,

shirt dampened from the strain
when the radiance of your face

surfaces in an openness, the sound
of your voice calling to me among

white blossoms of mountain laurel
that spread up the slope, with the clarity

of the phoebe saying its name
at the summit, where you recount

how we entered the house last night,
and our turning to kiss,

the petals from so many roses
dropping on the kitchen table.

Budding

We watched it bud into flower, and snow
fell through the months of darkness,

a vermillion gift, then petals dropped
a new bud underneath. Since the azalea

stopped blooming, we have begun to wither,
to cling tighter with the memory of budding.

Chrysanthemum

Its outer petals blend into a chiffon
that spirals to become a more intense

yellow at its center, as if its beauty
were already a memory, the negative

of a photograph held up to the light,
the hearty sweetness of its fragrance

a suggestion of something that is gone,
or going, the bouquet of autumn's

bright passing, now windblown through
the open window, dispersed in the air

that lingers, like the afterglow
of her in my arms this morning.

The Darkness Beneath the Pines

When darkness fell a mile
before we reached the trailhead,

our flashlight a wish
carried in the pack on my back,

I shuffled us through
dusty beds of pine needles,

using the toes of my boots
to guide us rock to rock,

wrenched my right knee trying
to feel the way down

one of the many drops of the path.
There was a crash through dry tinder;

you feared a bear, then silence,
our only light trailside orange fungi.

Hours later, when we arrived
in the glow of the parking lot,

you asked me to never tell anyone
how we nearly didn't make it back.

I find you again every time I cross
my left leg over the right knee:

the lingering pain a reminder
of us hobbling through

the darkness beneath the pines,
your left hand on my right shoulder

and right hand around my waist,
before, only a year later,

we will not be able to help
losing each other in the clear light of day.

The Departure

When he thinks of her on nights like this,
old rooms are no longer vacant,

her memory haunts trappings of furniture.
Someone has written her name in the dust.

On nights like this, what an imagination
decay has: the ceiling rolls back

its eyes, and he hears himself, like someone
distant, speaking to himself.

Duende

after Federico Garcia Lorca

Why this loss of self without disdain?
Oh, why such a swirl of golden leaves?

Why such a loss of disdain,
Especially on the road to Cordoba?

The flying hooves of horses *flamenco.*
And why the clouds? The wind crests

Each ridge like the bow over the strings
Of a cello, *Why me?,* without disdain,

And the road to Cordoba swirls
With golden leaves. Touch me then,

Daughter of glee, little sister midnight.
Oh, Cordoba, why me?

Your blinking eyes tease me beneath
the silver crescent of the moon —

But tonight, light my way. The road
To Cordoba glistens in the morning!

Double Rainbow

Walking the meadow track after
    a day of rain, beside the dripping
        trailside of autumn maples and oaks,

we enter into the mist descending
    and a shower of tamarack needles
        that turns golden in the twilight.

Only our angels know why we stop
    to look behind us into the sky
        to see the spread of the initial

prismed arc broadening its hues:
    each band distinguished in concentric
        patterns, when a second spectrum

appears curving above it—
    one reflecting the other
        across the horizon like flame.

We stand beneath it to watch
    the colors blaze, making me aware that
        we are reawakened by the wealth

of the continuum, that what we are now
    is what we always have been, that
        we were not meant to be too happy,

but we have grown into one another,
  walking as far as the hip deep swale,
    almost hovering there a moment.

Each Time

I think of you every morning when I awaken,
and you are not with me, how I would like

to kiss the shoulder closest to me,
then your forehead, and place my mouth

on your lips, as I did yesterday morning —
sunlight streaming into the studio

past the edges of the drawn shades.
I think of you every morning as you awaken,

how I would like to bend my face down to kiss
your face, both of us washed over with

the light of the April morning, not just
time after time but each time as if it is the first.

Electricity

What comforts him is to remember how they would listen
to thunder move in, from the porch, standing arm in arm,

how quickly waves of coolness began to clear
stifling summer air, how sheet after sheet of rain drove in

to flood gutters of the street, how tantalized they were
tingling in the force and shine of the storm.

The Evening Star

After bushwhacking a trail up
Mount Toby, we ascend

the fire tower at the summit;
our knees scuffed brown,

both of us gritty with dust.
You smile before removing

your top, soaked through from
the climb. Before we descend,

I kiss drops of sweat
from your skin, your redolence

fragrant with the scent of pine.
When I return to find the spot

we chose beside the path,
highbush blueberry

beginning to ripen with fruit,
I see your face again

in the dusk, and burning
above us, the evening star.

Every Morning

I wake up knowing she's
made a joke of my love,
and watch my hands shake
as if they were laughing.

Finding the Names of the Wildflowers Gone Past

I remember how I would name the wildflowers for you
on our walks together, as if I had gathered bouquet
after bouquet of them in your honor, and laid them
in your freckled hands, to mirror their beauty and yours.

I enunciated their names, with my lips and tongue,
as I would have placed a kiss on your lips. However,
the roadsides are no longer lined with blue chicory,
alias ragged sailor; the slopes of the meadow no longer

spill white with Queen Anne's lace; the yellow buttons
of the leafless corollas of tansy punctuate a short declarative
sentence reminding us of the brevity of summer;
and now the fringe of the meadow is abundant with

the purple of autumn asters; a wildflower that is
not only a harbinger of frost, but the color of my sorrow.

Gift

If I offer you a gift of a glass chrysanthemum
goblet filled with flat crystal seaglass-shape
gem stones, it is to charm the child within you;
and if I make a gift to you of rainbowed glass

within clear glass placed beneath a kiln-fired
glazed ceramic bowl, it is to respect
all of what we have held together, and that
we carry always. If I offer you reconciliation,

in the shining of glass and the luster of clay,
it is not just for us to become aware of what
holds its buff and polish, but to see the best
in each other, through which we may be able

to open in forgiveness of one another, and
begin to recognize ourselves and our shadows.

Green Silk Skirt

Passing the shop windows of a Sigrid Olson,
that is going out of business in Westport, we are

drawn in by the sign announcing the 70% off sale,
and walk across the cobbled street, where you find

your destiny in choosing that green silk skirt—
calling my name, after you put it on in one

of the changing rooms, and my calling your name,
before I draw the drapes aside to see how it looks—

both of us, unwittingly, electrifying the charm
of the elegant woman behind the desk into recounting

her three children, the eldest of whom just graduated
from high school, and who is on his way to college;

that she is divorced, but that *their Dad is a good
father,* as she rings in an extra 25% discount, so that

an $150 skirt is yours as my gift to you for under $35.
As I drive us home, you imagine what you will match

that green silk with, and how you might
compliment it with the white top you have that bears

the fabric trellis of white roses that climbs up
its right shoulder. When you offer me the present

of a fashion show after we return home, I spread
the breadth of my hands across the curves of your hips.

Guardian Angel

after Rolf Jacobsen

For years I have been trying to find the patience
to listen to the resonant whisper of her voice
tickling my ear. Sometimes I imagine I see her,

the one who keeps me calm, whose guiding hands
steer me out of the shallows of my own making;
who walks on a cool, dustless path; who presses

her head against my heart, whose arms around
my shoulders lift by morning; who awakens in me
a vision of the ruby in the hummingbird's song.

Heaven's Mountain

There is a myth
about a great love

in which a lover
marked his loved one so

that their scent
was preserved

in the fragrance
of the pines

on Heaven's Mountain,
and every time

the wind rocks
those branches,

the needles bristling,
sticky with sap,

we are reminded
of the inexplicable

sweetness and depth
of their passion.

Honey Locust

I always want to remember
her turning toward me to identify

its sweet fragrance on the wind,
as we stand together in stippled bands

of morning sunlight that flare
between the spiny branches

of its scaly trunk and white blossoms
through the opened bedroom window.

How many lives has it been?
How many years since we first met

in this life? I always want to remember
her turning toward me to ask

if I am able to distinguish its scent,
the knowing look on our faces,

as if no time had passed,
as if nothing had happened at all.

The Hundred Days of Summer

The drowsiness of the afternoon opens
    as the white flowers of water lilies
        close in direct sunlight.

Dragonflies settle on blackened
    stumps in the deadwood bog,
        a fritillary rides atop the flowers

of pickerelweed. We hike through
    glade after glade of club moss,
        the thrush's song stops us

mid-track, every phrase held in the air.
    We find the end of the trail
        on the banks of Mashapaug Pond,

nearly breathless from black flies,
    deerflies, mosquitoes, heat.
        After we swim, water hugs every

curve of you; as you dress
    behind me, I see your feet
        have printed the warm stones.

In You

If in you I see the projection
of my soul, I cannot help but think, *So that*

is how beautiful it is,
so that is how holy, so that is how deadly.

Kitchen Table

Always elegant
whenever lit with radiant

ears of sweet corn,
where drinking glasses

leave rings, where we
make commitments and

look out at the stars,
where sometimes on

Saturday night she places
a slender crystal vase

in the center
that contains the one

long-stemmed rose
I brought home.

Leaving

When I look out across the pasture at Larch Hill,
    this Saturday in mid-October, I think of how often
        we would walk here together, and talk to the herd

of cows, that would interrupt their grazing, and come
    to meet us by the electrified wire fence, huddled
        in their collective affection, tails swatting away flies;

and how we didn't quite want to leave that last time,
    in early September, but remained to stay, before going,
        to warm ourselves in the sun; and how I indicated

to you that farther up the cinder path, to the right,
    is where I would release prayers by the white pasture gate,
        to ask for guidance from the Lord. I have looked out

across the farmyard garden beyond, and over
    the weeks have observed that single maple tree,
        that overlooks the ridges of the Holyoke Range, turn

from green to crimson, then lose all of its leaves.
    Learn not to look for answers is what I have heard,
        and when I have been able to listen, *There is nothing*

that offers more grace than loving deeply. Upon our going,
    we passed a woman who was sitting on the wooden
        bench on the boardwalk, and when we walked by her,

I remarked to you, having been startled
     by the look on her face, that apparently, she must be
         struck with grief; but I believe the woman was not

an ordinary woman, but an angel, that appeared
     before us, and for what is the rest of our lives, watched,
         with such sadness in those eyes, our leaving paradise.

Luminous Dream

I can still feel the pull of her body toward mine
in the dream, afterward like the tide,

and hear her say: *No man has ever waited for me*
the way you have. You have waited like no other.

When we begin to work on cleaning
an Oriental rug, and we brush away layers of thick dust,

the design of the blue, green, and red feathers
of a Painted Bunting are revealed in the pattern

woven into the pile. The entire dream
unfolds in a lustrous light that is not only magnified

exponentially but also released as the bird is freed.
That occurs both in the dream and upon waking

on this plane. She will always be an incandescence
burning within me. What a journey the light has taken us on.

Lustre

The sky tonight, beginning to blossom
with constellations of spring, kindles me

to pause after work on the walk that glitters
with particles of icicles shattered by the fall

from the steep pitch of the shingled roof,
the same way the sparkle ignited in the eyes

of that herd of deer, frozen in headlight
beams for only an instant, in the first

blizzard of winter, crossing the road, quietly,
with such modesty, that they softened

the wild falling of the snow, and how
we reached over to the other in the darkness,

how our hands found the shape of touch,
as if we held the lustre of their starry eyes.

Maidenhair and Wild Roses

I found the note in the lunch
you had packed for me that read: *I love you.*

Remember this morning?
I did remember, standing beneath the cliffs

partway up the mountain—
those massive mossy alters lush with fern;

the emptiness at the center of a frond
of maidenhair, silky with a spider's web;

and in full bloom, a pair of the reddest
wild roses, growing from the same stem.

Not unlike you and I
when we give voice to passion, they intimated

sweet declaratives, trailing
a fragrance as rich as their color,

so thoroughly engaged they were,
as well as we, in the language of the heart.

Neruda

It is not impossible, or mutually exclusive,
for one person to love another:

one who is familiar with opulence
and one who understands what opulence is.

Once, you told me, Neruda
wrote about love as being unloosened

like seawater. Now when I think of you,
it is wave after wave of ocean I hear.

Never Tell a Woman

Never tell a woman over the phone
that you miss her at nine o'clock in the morning

just because you have slept together.
You miss me? she will say, as the telephone

leaps out of your hand into the air.
Shouldn't I miss you?, you will say,

braver than the brave. *I don't think it's
a question of shouldn't,* she will answer,

the telephone heavier than a loaded gun.
Never phone a woman at nine o'clock

in the morning, to tell her that you miss her,
but if you dare, and she says,

It both pleases me, and worries me,
you have the right number, but the wrong woman.

Open Song

Lover from a past life,
rose opening in a vase.

You haul on my desire
like a storm unfurls a banner.

My chest aches as if my heart
were stuffed with rags.

Lover shrouded in mist,
storm, opened rose.

Queen Anne's Lace

Every summer a specific species
    of wildflower has its season, spreads
        in abandon across the landscape, fills the meadows

from Mount Pollux to the highway's median strip,
    basks in the cracks of broken pavement buckling
        along Farmington Avenue in the restaurant district

of Hartford's West End to West Hartford's borderline.
    When you cut down two stems of Queen Anne's lace
        in the Berkshire Hills to exhibit elegance and strength

in nature, you are drawn to the parasol that leans
    into the coolness of evening, that nods in the rain,
        that remains open beneath the sun and the moon.

A whole field is a tapestry of flat white tops
    italicizing green meadow grass, sustained
        whimsy, silent applause. Walking the rise at dusk

after thunderstorms, we slosh
    through bedstraw, bladder campion, and fleabane,
        one of my hands riding on one of your shoulders,

to look south across the Holyoke Range, then north
    toward Pocumtuck and Toby, to watch the spirals
        of mist clear the sides of the ridges below early stars.

We do not want to let any of this go, spoken
    through loving, windblown wild carrot that roots
        in earth, and whose stalks rock in our summering.

Redbud

Walking beneath the flowering redbud
whose purple blossoms, you told me,

can be eaten and taste sweet,
I am not sure whether the fragrance

I inhale is that of your body
remaining with mine, and reminding me

of this morning after an evening
of love, or the petals of blossoms

blown from a branch that become a streak
of freshness on the wind, not unlike

the way you have marked me, with
such sweet surfeit, that I am yours.

The Ringing of Silence

They are not in any hurry, there are fewer expectations.
What is different this time is their stillness,

but not what is delicious about their familiarity.
They learn through the practice of separation

how to become more tender.
After she takes off her dress, she asks him

for one of his shirts, and he decides on the green corduroy.
She chooses to wear it unbuttoned.

All night, they qualify the difference
between holding on too tightly, and not holding on at all.

The Shower

After our night of love, we awaken with each other
to celebrate a morning of love. This will be one

of the days that we will not be able to contain
our happiness, and we will stop to kiss in the falling

snow when we walk North Pleasant Street in Amherst
to attend Saturday afternoon mass at Saint Brigid's.

It will be one of the days I will exclaim aloud that
I have never been any happier in my entire life,

one of the days when time will bend, and perpetuate
itself, apparently stop, the silver light of a February

afternoon, occasionally shining through clouds, and
you beside me, arm in arm, so much alive in whatever

we do, ecstatic, in our transcendent bump and grind
of hip to hip. This will be one of the days I will rise

from my side of the bed to walk around and lift you
by your hands, from your side, and we will step into

the shower together, and I will lather you in a stream
of water, the two of us wet with each other in the spray,

my hands gliding over your every curve — in abandon.
Before I soap the rose of your face, I ask you to close

those Mary Cassatt-sky blue eyes, then spread suds
over the aureoles of your breasts. When your hands

wash over me, only as a woman does who knows
her lover, your fingers do so as light that shines through

Marc Chagall-stained glass. We have never before
been as close. We have never been as cleansed.

Sacred Fire

The farther I travel up the trail,
I find myself becoming closer

to the unnamable, knowing
I am closer to the unnamable in you,

as if it were held in bands of sunlight
above the stream that flows with

heavy rain from the last days of June,
the way I held you, with a purity,

with no thoughts of anything else,
because nothing but you existed,

often with my eyes closed,
sometimes watching the light beneath

your skin flash across your face,
consumed this morning, as we were,

in the inextinguishable fire
our flesh and bones make sacred.

Snow Geese: A Mountain Poem

It is not the body
that lasts,
but the memories
of the body —
its consciousness,
the source
at the mountain's summit
rimmed blue with sky.

I want to share
all that I have
with you: my body,
the trail
up the mountain,
the wood asters
beside it,
the marsh hawk
shadowing the trail,
my kisses warming
you in the rain.

I walk the old roads
through these hills,
as if for the first time:

the pumpkin fields plowed under,
the sloping valley
cloaked in a shroud of smoke,

still rustling with
an abundance of crepuscular leaves
scoured and scoured in the wind . . .

out of my head with joy.

Why do I believe I knew you
before you existed?

Shimmering dew.
Riderless galloping horse.
Corn tassel.

Ridge after ridge
of rust red
maples and oaks
lulled into creaking
after a surge
of the wind.

The brush ticking
with the inimitable song
of the white-throated sparrow.

This road
through the late October hills.

❧

Years from now,
when we are gone
people will sense
and palpably perceive
the possibility that someone
walked here hand in hand

through a bright trail
of beech leaves
scuttling from berm to berm,

and picture,
shadow after shadow,
the flock of migrating snow geese

passing over us.

Summer Evening

She tries on old clothes: lace, secondhand
sweaters, wrinkled 50's dresses.

Sunbeams angle through the front windows,
and firecrackers explode

in the street where rush hour traffic
stalled hours ago. We don't say much.

I hardly touch her, but
we laugh and laugh and laugh.

The View Over Our Shoulders

You tell me how you see green
when I hold you in the garden,

on a path opening into woods,
and you look over my shoulder;

not unlike tonight when you see
our reflection in the kitchen window,

your head next to mine. I want us
to take care of our love for each other

the way we view a landscape,
an image over our shoulders, to see

ourselves as equals, not unlike
when you ask me to turn around

in the kitchen, to see our reflection
in the window, to see, when

you say: *Look. Do you see?*
Together. How beautiful.

Supplication in the Heart of Summer

after Andre Breton

The chiaroscuro of nuance,
the vowels of my wife's breath,

the soft drenching, the low
of the herd of Hereford across the field,

the light limning the pillow's edge,
the kiss of bird song, the vermouth of quiet,

the cusp of my wife's hands
holding a young rabbit,

the soft vowels of my wife's breath,
the beading rain jewelling lines

in the woods on the reeds,
the blankets of old wounds

bundled into the shape of a nap,
the arthritic legs of our old dog, his nose

wet with blossoms, the sweet scent
of hay always the handkerchief

of remembrance, the long road
sleepy with the tirelessness of distance,

the vowels of my wife's breath,
the embroidery of the angels,

the inhabitants of the grass,
the love we have that owned up to each other.

The Tide

Whenever I recall the lifetime
    I was a mariner, I see myself
        at a distance, as I look out

across the sea, returning
    with a cache of pearls in urns
        of delphinium blue, the deck

loaded with oysters in baskets
    of Tyrolean wicker.
        She had seen me off, centuries,

millennia ago, the purple ribbons
    in her hair blowing above her shoulders.
        I carried with me the memory

of the shape of her breasts, the taste
    of her skin burning on my tongue.
        Unable to navigate the unseen

reef in the channel, I was lost
    in a wreck, in a rush of waves, the hull
        splintering against rocks, my body

floating away among the deep-sea rooms,
    veil after veil of schools of passing fish
        fluctuating in trapezoidal walls.

When I recall my lifetime
    as a mariner, I watch her
        from a distance, as she looks out

across the sea, waiting —
    expecting me to be carried by the tide,
        to return to the harbor of her arms.

The Vision

He saw the pages rippling in the book
of their many nights of love, none alike,

beyond comparison, their salvation,
the deep dish of it, always unexpected

and without explanation, always
the unbelievable, long walks past fountains

where there were no fountains. Then, after
an undetermined number of years, his death,

the wind blowing through the open window,
the ten-year-old in him looking at her

in adoration, her hair now streaked
with silver, pinned back, as always,

with tortoiseshell barrettes, her blue eyes
peering out through a wisdom-map

of wrinkles, as he remembers her
in pink pajamas, leaning over the banister

in the rain, the driveway white with blossoms,
both of them uncupping blown kisses from

the palms of their hands, and reminding himself
how he thought he had no right to be this happy,

but if he could take it, this is what
it could be like for the rest of his life.

The Way Up the Mountain

Wrens, finches, and warblers
sing all the way up the mountain.

We identify wildflowers by the color
of their petals: the red spur

of columbine, the pale lavender
of wild geranium. This morning

we name our own flowering;
our voices rise in a chorus

above the hues of blossoms
in the meadow we step into —

the yellow, white, and purple
of wild oats, sarsaparilla, and trillium.

What He Tried to Tell Her Last Night in the Dark

is how he believes the soul
is a wafer of light,

how her soul and his
melt on their tongues in communion.

What I Saw on the Mountain

When you phone tonight, you ask me
to tell you what I saw on the mountain,

the scent of your body still fragrant
on mine, like furrows of wet moss

streaked with a trickle of the stream.
I tell you I saw the bull thistle's purple

flowers blooming within the shadow
of the cliffs, strands of goatsbeard

splayed above pink clusters of steeplebush
grown wild, a deadfall white pine, filling

the mouth of the gorge at the head of the falls,
whose gray branches flickered in the wind

like smoke. On top of the fire tower,
I watched bumblebees mate on a girder,

warm to the touch, above the corn
and tobacco fields in Sunderland,

the wind knocking acorns from
the rustling summit oaks. Then I saw

a scarlet tanager, whose inquisitive
song reminds me of tenderness,

and of the questions we ask each other
when we are close, the bright male

who flew by me, as a spotted doe
stepped out into a clearing with her fawn.

Witch-hazel

Walking with you on the trail
    through the sunlight slanting over the meadow,
        disappearing and reappearing

through the trees, never the same twice,
    but never more radiant than the light beneath
        the delicate bones of your face,

and your laughter warming
    this September morning, as you hold a yellow leaf
        from the tree named witch-hazel,

as we hold each other close once
    near noon, the fields still moist with dew,
        and the scent of autumn's decay beginning

to burn like a wick
    near the shoulders of the pond,
        and the blowing mist flaring across the face

of the ridge singed burnt orange
    and crimson, as I hold the memory
        of the meadow warm with your laughter,

and in holding this close,
    protect it like a sparrow cupped in a child's palms
        that turns his entire being into song.

Zebras

The black and white stripes blur
due to their quickness and what is tattooed

into the pigment of their hides by racing
through the grainy sands of the equatorial sun.

Who wouldn't intuit streams of their movement,
even before they wade through the pools

of water in the shallows of their quenching?
As they shake off the dust from

their tomahawk manes, they are never any happier
when they gallop over the dry banks of the channel

after they have plashed through river mud.
In this lifetime, when you mail a card to me,

signed, *Your Zebra,* with stripes
bearing themselves on the front cover,

and the smudge of your kiss a carnelian stamp
pressed onto the back of the envelope,

it makes your stallion whinny.
Whatever scent that you infused within

allows me to imagine how I would inhale
the aroma of your skin, as we stop in the wind

of our own making, among antelope and gazelle.
Let us run apart from the herd.

Let our stripes blend together
across the grasslands of the Savanna.

May we bask felicitously among irascible hippos.
And, *Oh, Darling,* may we outrun the lions.

Acknowledgments

The author is grateful to the editors of the following journals and anthologies in which these poems initially appeared, often in an earlier version.

America: "Supplication in the Heart of Summer"

Angel Face: "Finding the Names of the Wildflowers Gone Past"

Connecticut Review: "Honey Locust"

Foliate Oak Literary Journal: "Sacred Fire"

FutureCycle Poetry: "Double Rainbow"

Lady Jane's Miscellany (Online Extension): "The Shower"

Lalitamba: "The Tide"

The Larcom Review: A Journal of the Arts and Literature of New England: "The Anointing," "Chrysanthemum," "Guardian Angel"

Many Hands: A Magazine of Holistic Health: "The Way Up the Mountain," "Zebras"

The New Haven Advocate: "Summer Evening"

Old Crow: "Kitchen Table"

Osiris: "Heaven's Mountain"

Outerbridge: "Witch-hazel"

Puckerbrush Review: "The Hundred Days of Summer," "The Shower"

Rolling Stone: "Every Morning," "Open Song"

Ruminate: A Magazine of Faith in Literature and Art: "Queen Anne's Lace"

Sahara: A Journal of New England Poetry: "The Darkness Beneath the Pines," "Electricity," "Neruda," "The Vision," "What I Saw on the Mountain"

Spiritus: A Journal of Christian Spirituality: "Leaving"

Telephone: "Alone"

"Aftermath" originally appeared in an earlier version in *The Duchess of Malfi's Apricots and Other Literary Fruit* (Columbia, SC: University of South Carolina Press).

"And She Falls into My Arms Again" originally appeared in an earlier version in *Five Connecticut Poets* (Hamden, CT: Fireside Press).

"The Evening Star" and "The Way Up the Mountain" were collected in a limited edition letterpress volume published by Timberline Press (Fulton, MO).

"Gift" originally appeared in an earlier version in *The Light in Ordinary Things* (Berkeley, CA: Fearless Books).

"The Hundred Days of Summer" appeared in *Proposing on the Brooklyn Bridge: Poems About Marriage* (West Hartford, CT: Poetworks/Grayson Books).

"In You" originally appeared in an earlier version as a limited edition letterpress broadside issued by Bull Thistle Press (Jamaica, VT).

"Kitchen Table" was collected in *Hear a Poet, There a Poet* (Northampton, MA: Write from the Heart).

"Maidenhair and Wild Roses" and "Redbud" originally appeared in earlier versions in *Intimate Kisses: The Poetry of Sexual Pleasure* (Novato, CA: New World Library).

"Snow Geese: A Mountain Poem" originally appeared in an earlier version as a poem-in-a-pamphlet issued by Andrew Mountain Press (Hartford, CT).

Acknowledgment is made to the Connecticut Commission on the Arts for a fellowship in poetry that facilitated the writing of the initial drafts of some of these poems, early on.

Grateful appreciation is made to the Robert Francis Trust for awarding me two back-to-back one-year residencies at Fort Juniper, the Robert Francis Homestead, in Cushman, Massachusetts, where the drafts of some of these poems were composed, and on occasion, where the poems themselves were sometimes finished.

Cover art, "Morning on the river," by Joshua Havens (josh@jhavens.com)

Photograph of the author by Al Malpa (Willimantic Chronicle)

Cover design and typography by Diane Kistner (dkistner@futurecycle.org)

Poetry face, Book Antiqua

Books by Wally Swist

Books of Poetry

Luminous Dream (FutureCycle Press, 2010)
Veils of the Divine (Hanover Press, 2003)
The New Life (Plinth Books, 1998)
For the Dance (Adastra Press, 1991)*
New Haven Poems (Connecticut Fireside Press, 1977)

Poetry Chapbooks

Mount Toby Poems (Timberline Press, 2009)*
Waking Up the Ducks (Adastra Press, 1987)*
Of What We're Given (Dunk Rock Books, 1980)

Books of Haiku

The Silence Between Us: Selected Haiku (Brooks Books, 2005)
The Mown Meadow: First Selected Haiku & Sequences
(Los Hombres Press, 1996)

Haiku Chapbooks

The White Rose (Timberline Press, 2000)*
Train Whistle (Proof Press, 1996)
Blowing Reeds (Timberline Press, 1995)*
The Gristmill's Trough (Hummingbird Press, 1991)
Sugaring Buckets (High/Coo Press, 1989)
Unmarked Stones (Burnt Lake Press, 1988)*
Chimney Smoke (Juniper Press, 1988)*

Scholarly Monograph

*The Friendship of Two New England Poets,
Robert Frost and Robert Francis* (The Edwin Mellen Press, 2009)

*Indicates Letterpress Limited Edition

The FutureCycle Poetry Book Prize

FutureCycle Press conducts an annual full-length poetry book competition open to any poet writing in the English language. The winning manuscript is normally published over the summer, with the poet receiving a $1,000 prize plus 25 copies of the published book. Finalists may also be offered publishing contracts. Submissions of book manuscripts are accepted from January 1 to March 31 each year for that year's prize. The press also publishes individual poems in its online magazine, *FutureCycle Poetry*. These poems, which remain online indefinitely, are collected into an annual print edition each November.

To be considered, all submissions must be received via our online submission form. To avoid unnecessary delays or unread returns of submitted work, poets should review our guidelines:

www.futurecycle.org/guidelines.aspx

Poetry Books
from FutureCycle Press

FutureCycle Poetry Book Prize Winners

Stealing Hymnals from the Choir by Timothy Martin (2010)
No Loneliness by Temple Cone (2009)

FutureCycle Poetry Book Prize Finalists

Castaway by Katherine Riegel (2010 Finalist)
Simple Weight by Tania Runyan (2010 Finalist)
Luminous Dream by Wally Swist (2010 Finalist)
Beyond the Bones by Neil Carpathios (2009 Finalist)

Full-length Books

The Porous Desert by David Chorlton
Violet Transparent by Anne Coray

Chapbooks

The Secret Life of Hardware by Cheryl Lachowski
Colma by John Laue
Scything by Joanne Lowery
A Love Letter to Say There Is No Love
by Maria Russell-Williams

5883760R0

Made in the USA
Charleston, SC
16 August 2010